SONGS

BY
MARY
CAROLYN DAVIES

PUBLIC DOMAIN POETS

Editor: Dick Whyte   —: No. IV :—   April 2022

MARY CAROLYN DAVIES (**1888-1940?**) was born in the town of Sprague, moved to Portland as a child, and later went to Berkley University, where she became the first woman to win the Bohemian Club poetry prize, and the first freshman to win the Emily Chamberlain Cook Prize for Poetry. She left college after only a year, and moved to Greenwich Village, meeting poets and artists like Marianne Moore, Alfred Kreymborg, and Marcel Duchamp, among others. Best known for her rhymed poems, Davies was also an early practitioner of 'free verse' and wrote numerous unrhymed 'song' sequences, first published in Kreymborg's *Others: A Magazine of the New Verse* (1915-1919). During this time she was also a contributing editor for *The Occident, The Quill,* and later, *Voices.* Davies returned to Portland in the 1920s and became president of the Women's Press Club of Oregon, and the Northwest Poetry Society. In the 1930s Davies moved back to New York, but stopped publishing, and in 1940 the *Oregonian* reported that she had fallen seriously ill. It is likely that Davies died not long after this.

'Songs of a Girl I-XXIX' & 'Marriage Songs' ['The Proposal', 'Marriage', 'Wife', 'A Marriage'], published in *Youth Riding* (MacMillan, 1919); 'Songs I-XXIV' originally published in *Others: An Anthology of the New Verse* (1917). 'Other Songs' (1914-1920): 'Portrait' (*The Occident*, Sep. 1914); 'Songs of a Girl I-VIII' (*Others*, July 1915; *The New Poetry*, 1917); 'The Wild Wild Swans' & 'Songs' (*The Poetry Journal*, Feb. 1916); 'Later Songs I-VII' (*Others: An Anthology*, 1916) & 'Later Songs VIII-XI' (*Others*, April 1916); 'College' (*The Masses*, July 1916); 'Others I-IV' (Dec. 1917); 'Dance' (*Youth Riding*, 1919; *Poems of the Dance*, 1921); 'The Dancer', 'Restaurant Tables', & 'A Greenwich Village Tea Room' (*The Stratford Journal*, Oct. 1918; *The Drums In Our Street*, 1918; *Youth Riding*, etc.); 'Ambition' & 'Also' (*A Pagan Anthology*, 1918); 'Forest Dance' [first stanza] (*Youth Riding*, 1919); 'A Day I-VI' (*Poetry*, Aug. 1917; *Youth Riding*, 1919); 'Words' (*The Quill*, Feb. 1918), 'City Lights' (Mar. 1918), 'Monterey' (April 1918), 'A Garden', & 'Comrade' (June 1918), 'The Jest', & 'Summer Night' (July 1918), 'A Bullet' (Oct. 1918), 'Rebel' (Nov. 1918), 'Stars' (Feb. 1919), & 'Miracles' (Feb. 1920). Afterword: 'The Poet' [edited] (*The Poetry Journal*, March 1916).

Cover: Maude Langtree – 'Through the Arch' [& 'Sullivan Street'], & William Zorach – 'Eve' (*The Quill*, 1917-1918). Inside: Louise Helene Caldwell – 'Branches' (*Outdoors & Us*, 1922); 'Flower' (*Golden Songs of the Golden State*, 1917); Chester A. Reed – 'Swan' (*Illustrated Bird Dictionary*, 1912), Arthur Young – 'Woman's Portrait' (*The Masses*, April 1916); Hegara – 'Dancers', & Wood Gaylor – 'Dressing Room' (*The Quill*, 1918). etc.

PUBLIC DOMAIN PRESS

Aotearoa / New Zealand

ISBN: 978-0-473-62866-6 (print) • 978-0-473-62867-3 (kindle)
978-0-473-62868-0 (pdf)

MARY CAROLYN DAVIES
SONGS OF A GIRL & OTHER VERSES

SONGS OF A GIRL

A sequence of 29 songs, written 1915-1919.
This version first published 1919.

MARRIAGE SONGS

'The Proposal', 'Marriage', 'Wife', & 'A Marriage'.
First published 1919.

SONGS

A sequence of 24 songs, written 1915-1917,
some of which later appeared in 'Songs of a Girl'.
This version first published 1917.

OTHER SONGS

A selection of other songs & variants.
Published 1914-1920.

SONGS OF A GIRL

from
YOUTH RIDING

1919

SONGS OF A GIRL

I

The buds
Coming to color
Make me weep.
For my own brown cloak
Has never been broken.
Spring, rend me!

II

The hummings of the street,
Their whisperings,
And the moon
White above me —
These, and the beating of my heart
Make me glad —

III

The moon
Strikes my hand
Across my face as I lie.
And the pain of it
Keeps me from sleeping.

IV

Rainsound, sunset, and night,
Clear skies, and the falling of water —

Who would seek love?

V

What is love?

Love is when you touch me,
Love is the noise of stars singing as they
    march,

Love is a voice of worlds glad to be together.
What is love?

VI

There is a strong wall about me to protect me,
It is built of the words you have said to me.

They are swords about me to keep me safe,
They are the kisses of your lips.

Before me goes a shield to guard me from harm,
It is the shadow of your arms between me and danger.

VII

We walked alone through the long corridors
    of living,
Our footfalls echoing;
And then we came
By opposite doors
To the great hall
Of each other's presence.

VIII

For long
Locked shields within me
Withstood the onslaught of your words.
Then came your kiss
Like an arrow shot cunningly upward —

IX

See, I lead you to my heart.
It is a winding way, the way to my heart,
It is thorn beset and very long,
It is walled and sentineled,
And none could ever find the way alone.
So take my hand, and I will lead you to my
heart.

x

Touch me, and I am yours.
I do not know why —

XI

Your kiss
Is on my face
Like the first snow
On bewildered grass —

XII

Your hand and mine
Hold converse together.
We do not know what they are saying.

Although we listen,
Eager eavesdroppers,
We cannot understand
What they are saying —

XIII

I feel your heart beating in your hands as they
     touch me;
I feel your breath
Sobbing against my hair.
Oh, put your mouth on mine and leave it so —

XIV

That leaning tree was once a girl, and heard
A man's heart next her own. Remembering
She holds her arms across the moon for us —

XV

Our hearts lie so close
   That when your heart trembles
    Mine will be afraid.

Our hearts beat so near
   That when your heart stirs
    Mine will hear it.

Our hearts speak so loud
   That all the world must know —

XVI

Of sticks and leaves
We made an image of love
In play.
And then the image came to life
And seized us —

XVII

We two — we are young!
We have lips to sing,
To sing and kiss.

We two, we are glad!
We have hearts that beat,
That beat — and break.

XVIII

Take this kiss and wear it,
A shield that will ward off
My words that might hurt you —

XIX

Within the little house
Of my great love for you,
This safe and happy house,
I sit and sing, while all the world goes by.

Within the house that is my love for you
No harm can come, nor any thought of fear;
There is no danger that can cross the
threshold.

You did not build this house
Nor I;
But God the Carpenter —

XX

Your eyes are two miracles,
And I who have seen them,
Believe.

XXI

Perhaps
God, planting Eden,
Dropped a seed
Within Time's neighbor plot
That grew to be
This hour?

XXII

Like an artist
Who had finished a masterpiece
And is almost afraid,
You passed your finger
Tremblingly
Over my lips
Outlining their curves
In the darkness.
And when you felt them smile
You kissed the smile out
And forced hunger upon them —

XXIII

The moments
Of our being tired of one another
Are the whetstone
Against which Life holds
The knife of our loving.

XXIV

Your arms can speak
More readily than your voice.
Your shoulder touching mine tells breathless
    news.

XXV

Birds,
And leaves falling in Autumn,
Have tried to teach me sadness,
But they have only taught me joy.
Perhaps it is you,
Come to bring joy to me,
Who shall show me sadness at the last?

XXVI

I hear our hearts together
Like one clock
Ticking our lives away.
Could not some other
Have reminded us of death?
Why must it be
Our own hearts
In the first hour
That they have beat together?

XXVII

Life is a dagger
With no hilt.
As you tighten your arms about me
You only drive the two ends deeper
Into your heart
And mine.

XXVIII

I bend and touch the torches in your eyes;
Their flame lights all the little room called
    life.

XXIX

The wonder of your arm about me,
Of your face close enough to touch,
Of your soft breathing —

What can God show me
When I am dead
That can make me marvel?

MARRIAGE SONGS

from
YOUTH RIDING

1919

THE PROPOSAL

The carved chair is angry with me.
See how straight and stiff it is;
It disapproves
Because I have on my green slippers
And because I have danced a hole in my
    stocking,
And perhaps, too, because I am happy.

The mirror loves me;
And so I bend to kiss it
Where my own lips show leaning to meet me.

The mirror understands
Because it has seen into the hearts of many
women,
And I shall be a woman soon.

Swaying curtains, you are not more beautiful
Than I,
You are not more graceful
Nor does the wind curl its fingers about you
    more readily.

You sway and dream.
Even so do I sway in the wind of life, and
    dream —

Fire on the hearth,
That do you know?
I am very young,
And you have lived through the ages.
Tell me.

— But perhaps I would not believe, after
all —

Great carved lions
Over my mantel
You have guarded me well.

Portrait of a kissed lady,
Portrait of a man who is growing old,
Portrait of a child who would rather be
    playing —

Portraits of dead people,
Do you live again when you see me?
Do you remember, too?

Square ceiling,
You have kept the sky from me for a long
    time,
But now I have found the sky.

Walls, your arms have held me close,
But soon other arms shall hold me.

Shadows playing in the room,
Leaping, clutching at one another,
You are too young to understand.

Romp, shadows!
When the fire goes,
You shall not play any more —

MARRIAGE

Back from the dusty church,
The words all said
And the strange kiss given,
We walked down the long lane of Fourteenth
    Street,
(Our shoulders touching home-bound clerks,
And shoppers, straggly shawls about their
    heads),
To the Hungarian restaurant where for
    weeks
You had courted me between the soup and
    steak.

To-night
The mirrors all about the walls seemed only
To show your face to me, and mine to you;
Wherever I might look, I found your eyes,
You mine, and as we gazed
We quite forgot that earth held other things;

Until our friendly waiter, twinkling-eyed,
Came bustling back, a link from heaven to
    earth.

Three blocks of windy street,
Three flights of stairs,
And then we stood
Before your studio door.
You turned the key
And groping in the dark, you found a candle
And pouring tallow in a little pool
Upon the mantelpiece, you stood it there
In its tall whiteness.

There was rain outside;
The skylight hummed and rattled with its
    coming.
A few faint sounds blew up from the loud
    distance;

The grunt of a Salvation Army's drum
Blent with the noise
Of women's voices roughened by the night
Singing from hearts the night has roughened
        too —
And softened.

The street flung up its sounds against our
    window,
But could not force the fortress of our
    thoughts,
Your thoughts of me, and mine of you, old,
    new,
And riotous —
And frightened —

We, who had always been such
    open comrades,
Now were half afraid
To touch each other's hands,
To see each other's faces in the dim
And holy dusk.

We thought of God.   I prayed to Him,
As I had prayed when first you said, " I love
    you,"
The same quick, breathless, little broken
    prayer,
" God, oh, don't let us hurt each other, ever."

The portraits you had painted were about us,
A ghostly company of friends.
Life seemed all ends;
Ends of things finished, ends of things begun,
Ends, ends —
No safe and placid middles.

Because the silence choked from utterance
All other words, we talked of daily things,
Your order for a cartoon, and the story
Long overdue, that I must mail to-morrow —

And then the silence
Laid its hands even on these commonplaces.

We looked at one another gravely,
Shy children that our mothers, Youth and
    Life,
Had brought to see each other, and to play
Together.

Two startled children
Permitted by the gold ring on my hand
To stay and talk there in the dusk alone
And for the first time not to think of clocks
But if we liked, watch night's dark bud bloom
    dawn.

The silence grew and filled the room's dim
corners.

The candle on the mantel burned its life out
And its flame died, and all the room was
    dark;
And on the skylight fell the black loud rain;
And in the world there was no other sound
But your breathing
And the beating of my heart.

Then in the dark
You stumbled to me
And caught me by the shoulders
And laid your mouth on mine.

And all the hunger of our lives for life,
And all my hunger for you, yours for me,
Surged up in us, love caught us as a storm
A helpless ship, and beat upon us; joy
Rose like a tossing sea, and swallowed us.

WIFE

You are a rope
That binds me to a desk,
That ties me by the wrist
To its chair.

They two,
The desk and chair
Alone of all the world
Hear my ideals
And my beliefs
And my thoughts about things.
In the window.
There is a sky
With roofs denting it.

Under the roofs are the people
Who ought to hear
What the two
The desk and chair
Greedily lap up.

— I do not love the desk and chair
It is the rope that makes me talk to them.

A MARRIAGE

Walking along a mountain trail at night
 with you,
Never knowing when a rock will turn be-
 neath our feet
Or the loose earth slip
And plunge us into the half-seen precipice
 below —
Our life is like that.
We cling to each other's hands tightly;
We walk cautiously;
And are too frightened
To be unkind.

SONGS

from
OTHERS

1917

I

The buds
Coming to color
Make me weep.
For my own brown cloak
Has never broken.
Spring, rend me!

II

The hummings of the streets,
Their whisperings,
And the moon
White above me —
These, and the beating of my heart
Make me glad —

III

The moon
Strikes her hand
Across my face as I lie.
And the pain of it
Keeps me from sleeping.

IV

Red as dawn
The apple petals burn
Against my burning cheek.

V

Rainsound, sunset, and night,
Clear skies, and the falling of water —

Who would seek love?

VI

Your kiss
Is on my face
Like the first snow
On bewildered grass —

VII

Your hand and mine
Hold converse together.
We do not know what they are saying.

Although we listen,
Eager eavesdroppers,
We cannot understand
What they are saying —

VIII

That leaning tree was once a girl, and heard
A man's heart next her own.   Remembering
She holds her arm across the moon for us —

IX

Of sticks and leaves
We made an image of Love
In play.
And then the image came to life
And seized us —

X

Clutching at immortality,
We found each other's hands.

XI

Take your arms away
That I may remember their pressure. —

XII

My hand is blind without you —

XIII

We two — we are young!
We have lips to sing
To sing and kiss.

We two, we are glad
We have hearts that beat
That beat — And break.

XIV

Take this kiss and wear it,
A shield that will ward off
My words that might hurt you —

XV

The sun is a fire in the sky
And the thought of you
Is a fire in my heart.

The gray sea
Will quench the sun —

XVI

As if life were a fruit
And you
The only tree on which it grew

XVII

The moments
Of our being tired of one another

Are the whetstone
Against which Life holds
The knife of our loving.

XVIII

Your arms can speak
More readily than your voice
Your shoulder touching mine tells breathless news.

XIX

Birds
And leaves falling in Autumn
Have tried to teach me sadness
But they have only taught me joy.
Perhaps it is you
Come to bring joy to me
Who shall show me sadness at last?

XX

I hear our hearts together
Like one clock
Ticking our lives away.
Could not some other
Have reminded us of Death?
Why must it be
Our own hearts
In the first hour
That they have beat together?

XXI

Life is a dagger
With no hilt.
As you tighten your arms about me
You only drive the two ends deeper
Into your heart
And mine.

XXII

Now as we hear
The little sobbing words
Half yours, half mine —

XXIII

I bend and touch the torches in your eyes
Their flame lights all the little room called Life.

XXIV

The wonder of your arm about me,
Of your face close enough to touch,
Of your soft breathing —

What can God show me
When I am dead
That can make me marvel?

OTHER
SONGS

1914 – 1919

Portrait

She is so brave;
She is so wonderful;
Her eyes are glad.

She is so true;
And full of sympathy,
She has no fear.

And is she beautiful?
How should I know?

SONGS OF A GIRL

I

There is a morning standing at my window, looking
   into my room, and saying:
        " What will you do with me?
        I am your slave
        I will bring to you whatever you wish
        Only tell me what you want me to do
        And I will do it,
        What you want me to bring to you
        And it is yours."
And with a sudden rush of tears to my heart, I said:
        " Oh, morning, I do not want anything.
        There is something I want, oh, very much!
          But I do not know what it is exactly.
          Perhaps to die — perhaps to live —"

II

I am not afraid of my own heart.
I am not afraid of what may be in the places where
　the shadows are piled.
I am not afraid — see, I walk straight in
And look everywhere.
I am not afraid — ah, what was that?

It is a dangerous place in which to walk — a heart.
Especially one's own.

III

Just to be young
Young enough to laugh when one should weep —

IV

There are three of us; the little girl I used to be, the girl I am, and the woman I am going to be. We take counsel together concerning what colors we shall weave into the dream that we are making.

Sometimes they say, she is day-dreaming,
They do not know that we are taking counsel together, the little girl, and the girl I am, and the woman that I am going to be.

There are many things that they do not know.

V

I was alone with just me, the other evening
The me that nobody else knows
The me that is the nicest person I have ever met.
(Oh, quite the nicest!)

I was alone with just me
We had much to talk over
We had never properly met before,
But only caught glimpses
(Sometimes we were sure we wanted to meet, and at
    other times we hoped that we never would)
We had all the years before to discuss and all the
    years after to talk about
And there were other things — ourselves, and what
    life was — Oh, we had much to talk over.
So we sat there, silently, and did not say a word.

VI

The little kiss is trembling on my lips
        It will not leave its home, it is afraid.
"Go, go," I whisper, but it weeps and stays.

The little kiss is restless on my lips
        "Nay, I must go," it whispers, "I must go,"
"Ah, wait a little, wait," I counsel, "wait"—

VII

A turn of a stranger's head
Sometimes brings you very near to me.
A color,
A sound,
And I hear your breathing;
I feel your eyes upon mine.
A room darkened for the death of a day,
And I weep for you;
A bird crying out its song against its neighbors',
A flower new-born, startled —
And my heart beats with joy of you —

You whom I never knew
Whom I only loved.

VIII

I am going to die too, flower, in a little while—
Do not be so proud.

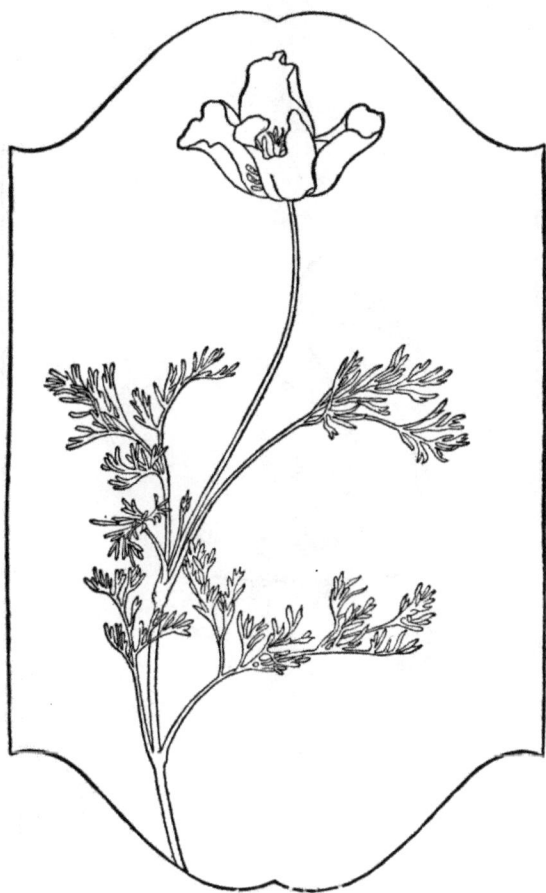

THE WILD, WILD SWANS

I heard in my sleep
The wild, wild swans
Flying,
Flying through the night,
And I moaned
And awoke
And the white moon
Stared soberly in
Through the window.

SONGS

White wild morning-glories
Are around her feet
And birds somewhere
Speak of her friendly wise among themselves.
Shadow of white things make her,
      and sun and a little sweetness
White morning glories are in her hands
And there is a wild bird prisoned in her throat
A brid that sings,
Of sweetness is her mouth made;
And her breatst are two white dreams—

If I could put my love to you in a little song
You would wear it proudly.
Oh that my heart could be
A ruby upon your throat
A ruby upon a thread of gold
To rise and fall with your breathing.
If I could show to you my soul
You would see as in a mirror
Your face—

You are not real,
You are perfect beauty,
And perfect beauty is a dream.

You are my dream.
See, I will shut my eyes so that you may not go away.
You are my dream.
I would close my eyes in death if that would keep you.

Give me your lips; I would live.
Let me feel the beating of your blood,
Let me hear your heart speaking my name.
Your hand in mine—
A lark in the earth,
A bud in its sheath,
A maiden in her room.

When your head is on my breast
I am a conqueror,
I am one with a sword
Battling for you.

When my head rests on your bosom
I am a man who has found God,
A runner who has won to the goal,
A striver who has attained.

Give me your lips—
I would live—

Your eyes are two miracles;
And I, who have seen them,
Believe.

LATER SONGS

I

The one who gives them out is short of dreams
With jealous husbandry
He deals them carefully
One dream to every two people
" You must share it
We're short of dreams," he says
But they
Are only glad of the excuse of sitting down
To the same dream ——

II

Perhaps
God, planting Eden,
Dropped, by mistake, a seed
In Time's neighbor-plot,
That grew to be
This hour?

III

You and I picked up Life and looked at it curiously
We did not know whether to keep it
                        for a plaything or not
It was beautiful to see, like a red firecracker
And we knew, too, that it was lighted.

— We dropped it while the fuse was still burning —

IV

The careful ocean sews
Pools, like round blue buttons
On the gray coat of the sand.

V

A wave heaps
Green tangled ribbons of sea-weed
On the gray counter of the sand
Then it rushes away
Like a salesgirl when the gong sounds.

VI

The sun is dying
Alone
On an island
In the bay.
Close your eyes, poppies!
— I would not have you see death
You are so young —

VII

Whose passing foot
Disturbed this ant-hill?

VIII

The sun falls
Like a drop of blood
From some hero.

We,
Who love pain,
Delight in this.

IX

I waited upon a hill for the sunrise.
(It was a very little hill.)
I waited for the sunrise.
In the chill dark I waited.

And in the cool gray before any dawn.
I waited for the sunrise,
With lips apart to praise.

But when it came it was a very old sunrise,
And I went away weeping.

X

You are calling upon me,
Fashionably clothed,
Properly prepared with small talk.
I sit sedately and help build up
The stone wall between us,
   with my little bricks of yes
      and no.

There are hothouse flowers on the table,
New York is outside the window—and inside—

The housemaid
has set the chairs
as carefully in their spheres
as God could ever
have placed the stars

Within the grate
There is a fire burning,
It has nearly gone out.

It is only a smouldering red thing now.

But as we look at it
Suddenly ages crumple,
The room vanishes,
You and I are a man and woman in a cave
With fire—

XI

Take what the gods give.
Tomorrow may be Monday on Olympus.

OTHERS

I

The moon is a girl
Riding a white pony
Over the gray sagebrush
Of the sky;
The stars are frightened white rabbits
That run across the path in front of her.

II

The moon is a silver fish;
The tall pine has caught it
In the net of its flung branches
And stands watching its struggles
And waiting for it to die.

III

The clouds are sea-gulls
Flying over the ocean of the sky;
The moon is a lighthouse,
And the white-bodied clouds
Beat their gray wings against it.

IV

From one of the branches
Of the magnolia tree
In our garden
It is large and creamy and fragrant;
It is the first flower of the year.

The other buds are angry
Because it has opened first.

Buds, do not be angry!
For it will wither
And fall
Before the morning——

COLLEGE

FIRST I became
   A copy of a book.

Then I became
A copy of a man
Who was also
A copy of a book.

Now
I would not know
What I am

Except that I have
On my wall
A framed paper
Which explains it fully.

Dance

God's in me when I dance.
God, making Spring
Out of his thoughts
And building worlds
By wishing.
God
Laughing at his own
Queer fancies,
Standing awed,
And sobbing;
Musing,
Dreaming,
Throbbing;
Commanding;
Creating —
God's in me
When I dance.

The Dancer

I watch the dancer,
Bending,
Lithely stooping,
Leaping, rippling,
Her motions changing
As though she were a song
  of many notes;
Her white robes swaying,
Her scarves like water under wind;
Her face held up to joy
As a leaf to sunlight;
Her arms yearning
  and crying out for beauty,
Reaching up
And pulling down beauty
  upon her head,
Then flinging it from her,
     to our outstretched hands.

But it is you
Calm, restrained, motionless,
Sitting beside me in your orchestra
    seat, watching her also.

It is you whom I see dancing
    with such ecstasy,
Tortured with music
Mad with motion
Giving yourself to your joy;
It is your throat, upon whose
    whiteness the light falls,
Your transfigured face I see
Held up to gladness
As a leaf to sunlight,
And your lifted arms
Asking, and holding beauty.

You
Seeing my tranced eyes fixed upon her
Are a little jealous.
— You need not be,
Beloved.—

RESTAURANT TABLES

The little tables in restaurants
That are made for lovers to talk across,
The eager little tables
Would have much to tell each other
If they could meet.

Some have seen a kiss
Given in a glance.
Others have seen moments made
Which will last forever.

A red, mother-of-pearl table in San Francisco
On which rest two cups without handles,
And on which tea is spilt,
Could tell of young lovers quarreling,
And with rude, quick, hands
   breaking all their sweetest memories
So that the bitterness inside oozes forth.

A table in an uptown hotel
Stiff with crystal and cut flowers,
Prim with an array of forks and glasses
Seeming placed in their spheres
   by the music that is near,
Could tell of words like budding seeds
Breaking through the hard
   frozen ground of youth
And springing to sudden sunlight.

And the little rough wooden table
In George's on Sixth Avenue
Knows what you said to me
Last evening.

A GREENWICH VILLAGE TEA ROOM

The dingy basement restaurant
Where the artists used to come —

The little smoky room
Where the artists sat
Blowing dreams from their cigarettes,
Shaping them with their lips
And watching them rise and die
      with equal languor —

The little smoky room
That has known tragedies
In many young men's eyes,
Has seen births,
And deaths —

The little smoky room
Is empty now —

On a spring night,
War sauntered into it
Casually,
And the young men linked
their arms in his,
And marched out through the door
Singing, and laughing,
and jesting with their
new comrade.

"ALSO."

Could that man ever have seen the stars,
That sacred historian who added,
As a careless afterthought,
Scrawling it down, perhaps, in the margin for
    insertion,
"He made the stars also—"?

AMBITION

The little fire
On the hearth
Dreaming of forests
Where it will
One day
Race and sing,—

And we before it
Dreaming.

I SHALL dance in the forest,
     And all my dancing shall be for you—
For you, who are very far away.

A DAY

I

SUN PRAYER

Sun,
Lay your hand upon my head.
I shall be kind to-day.
Sun, make me kind!
And lovely too —
My eyes,
And cheeks.   And make me wise.
I bow my head
Low, low —
Lay your hand upon it, so.

II
SHADOWS

Lean lower, Tree!
Give your beauty all to me.

Have two arms to reach the sky.

Eyes I have
And hands to press
Lazy buds apart, and feet
To touch the stream with,
Mouth to sing
And ears to hear the gray brook's tone.
These I have, these only.   Tree,
Give your shadows all to me!
I have no shadows of my own.

III
WIND PRAYER

Tree-wind
Sea-wind
Wind that whirls the sand,
Loud wind
Cloud wind
Wind of swaying water,
Let me hold your hand,
Let me be your daughter!

Give me what I need,
Wind of leaf and seed —
Say your magic wisdom
Over, slow, to me,
Wind that rules the sea!
Wind that rules the grasses!

— The wind passes —

IV
RAIN

Rain falls on the grass
And on my feet.
The drops are cool and round. The
    clover, oh
How sharp it greets me !   And the trees
    bend low
Beneath the raindrops.

Faster
Louder
Rounder
Colder
The mad drops strike.

If we were older
We should be wise and shrink from rain.
But because we are young, the grass and I
Hold out our arms for its pain.

V
THE GRAPES

The grapes are round and dark
Like eyes that mark
Each thing I do.
The sun has made them sweet and round;
The wind will pull them to the ground.
— I shall die, too.

VI

DUSK

Dusk,
Wrap your mantle
About us both.
I am tired too,
And cold, and full of sleep.

And keep
Your arm around me.   Day
Is far away
And night has not yet called us.
Let us pull
The mantle closer, Dusk, O beautiful!

A BULLET

Like a bird
You flew over the sweet summer fields;
Like a homing bird,
And nestled in his heart.

REBEL

I do not want to be a leaf
When I am dead;
Or a red rose.
I must, though, I suppose!

MIRACLES

To be alive,
And to have you for a friend,
These are two miracles
In a world of commonplaces.

* * *

SUMMER NIGHT

The moon
Strikes her hand
Across my face as I lie,
And the pain of it
Keeps me from sleeping.

CITY LIGHTS

The little lights that spring to fight the dark,
Then sleep, and wake next night to strive again—
They yet may sometime slay the dark—
                        who knows?

WORDS

Our hearts
Were comrades from the first;
But, ah, our words!
Like enemies they clashed and hacked and cut,
Like foes they answered thrust with thrust,
Our words, that parted us.

A GARDEN

A garden is the earth remembering
Her Eden time. Each flower is a regret,
Or flash of pride, or half-forgotten hope,
The memory of some passing word of God's
Or glance, perhaps——

MONTEREY

The adobe houses,
Bullied by the winds,
Give up their beauty,
But cling jealously to their memories.
The crumbling tiles are mindful of the past.
The mission bell calls to them all:
Remember!
Far out
The fishing boats
Fly like white moths,
Where the candle of the sun
Is set low upon the sea rim.

THE JEST

Someone put a moon in the sky
To tempt me.
I reach my hands up stealthily for it in the dark,
But there are eyes watching,
And when I draw back in fear
The eyes twinkle.

★　★　★

STARS.

Vain little stars,
You stand all day
Trying to make us look at you!
And, now, it is night,
You wag your heads boastfully at each other
Because you have succeeded.

COMRADE

I am glad that you love me.
It is only the love of a comrade,
I know,
But after wild loves
And fevered,
It is very good, this love of a comrade.
It will not change.
I shall fail,
And do foolish things;
I shall stumble,
And you will not be ashamed of me;
You will love me still;
You will always care
About what life is doing to me.
There will be no possession in your love,
There will be no beating of pulses;
Only a caring
And a being glad with me,
And sorry, too;
Only a standing by
And a steadying of the hand sometimes.
Love me so,
Comrade.

THE POET

MARY CAROLYN DAVIES

The poet is the only one who goes through the world without a shield. They are the only one who has no citadel of secrecy into which to withdraw themselves. There are no hidden rooms in their heart; it is thrown open to all, to trample as they will. Others live behind walls, the poet lives exposed to every blast.

In poetry the poet bares their heart that we may watch it beat; they give themselves that we may be saved. A poet is of use to the world only as they cast aside all walls of reticence and gives all that they feel, frankly to every comer. If they are hurt they cannot creep away to suffer in solitude; they must leave the wound open for all to see.

We are like surgeons experimenting on vagabond hearts of poets in order to know how to save our own carefully nurtured hearts. We look into the poet's exposed heart to find out what is in our own. We are interested in their suffering only as it may save us from suffering ourselves.

The poet who does not write from their own heart, who does not give us themselves freely, frankly and bravely,   is but an echo. The true poet holds back nothing from people, they hold out to them all that they have. Their gift to the world is themself.

The poet must be many-sided; they must love many different things so that they can speak to all people. The more things that stir them, waken them to rapture and force them to high moods, the better they can trumpet us to greater life.

The poet who lives greatly will write greatly. The

poet must keep themselves from petty things. They must be impervious to small hurts, to cares and worries; their mind must be open, not to the little thing that is near, but to the great thing, whether far or near.

Above all, the poet should be glad. There is a haunting sadness and beauty in melancholy, but no one can prove that there is not at least as much beauty in gladness. It has been the trend of the past to find its most exquisite beauty in sadness; its songs have been in a minor strain; but   it is the trend of this new age to search for the beauty of gladness, that is so much harder to find . . .

Youth and joy at last are coming into their own, and it is the poet who must set them surely upon their high throne. Every sad thought that wins us does so only because it has somewhere in it a hint of gladness. It is the thread of pleasure woven through pain that holds our hearts.

The poet should make it their life-long business to train themselves for the creation of beauty. This and this alone is their vocation. They must learn to see beauty in what someone trained for humorous writing would see humor only; in what a pessimist would see despair only. They must find beauty where beauty is and where beauty is not; and they must so rearrange what they have seen and heard and felt as to create from them a new loveliness.

Of all forms which beauty takes, words are the only form that lives. The poet who creates the most beautiful thing in words gives the world something with which the work of no states-person, warrior, or scientist can compare.

For that poet who can catch
in a cage of words the bird of beauty,
immortality waits.

In giving up the fortress of restraint and reticence, which even the poorest holds, the poet loses much, but by turning all that comes to them into song they gain. A grief given perfect expression in words holds as much of joy as it could have held of pain. A pleasure given perfect expression in words becomes ecstasy. The joy of the creator who feels that they are not working alone, that beauty is lending them aid and is with them in all they do, belongs to the poet.

To a poet trained to see beauty in all things life takes on a wholly different aspect. Every day is an adventure in joy; every mood is a new world to explore and to give to those who wait. Death becomes not a doom, but an opportunity. It is the poet, self-trained for ecstasy, who knows life at its greatest and most wonderful.

And what person may not
claim joy for themselves?

What person
may not see beauty?

What person may not be a poet?

> This Space for Your
> Thoughts

Please handle with care.

www.ingramcontent.com/pod-product-compliance
Lightning Source LLC
La Vergne TN
LVHW041321080426
835513LV00008B/534